TROMBONE

PLAY ALONG WITH THE CANADIAN BRASS

15 INTERMEDIATE PIECES

CANADIAN BRASS

Trumpets: Ryan Anthony, Joe Burgstaller
Horn: Jeff Nelsen
Trombone: Gene Watts
Tuba: Chuck Daellenbach

To access companion recorded performances and
accompaniments* online, visit:
www.halleonard.com/mylibrary

Enter Code
1582-2527-7707-6814

The part remains faintly on the recordings for guidance.

Recorded 2001, Toronto; Rob Tremills, engineer

ISBN 978-0-634-04973-6

HAL•LEONARD®
7777 W. BLUEMOUND RD. P.O. BOX 13819 MILWAUKEE, WI 53213

Visit Hal Leonard Online at
www.halleonard.com

Visit Canadian Brass online at
www.canadianbrass.com

ANDANTE
from the Trumpet Concerto

Joseph Haydn
(1732-1809)
arranged by Walter Barnes

PRAYER
from *Hansel and Gretel*

Engelbert Humperdinck
(1854-1921)
arranged by Henry Charles Smith

TROMBONE

RONDEAU

Jean-Joseph Mouret
(1682-1738)
arranged by Walter Barnes

TROMBONE

CANON

Johann Pachelbel
(1653-1706)
arranged by Walter Barnes

TROMBONE

WHERE'ER YOU WALK

from *Semele*

George Frideric Handel
(1685-1759)
arranged by Walter Barnes

In a singing manner; ♩ = 96

PILGRIMS' CHORUS
from *Tannhäuser*

Richard Wagner
(1813-1883)
arranged by Henry Charles Smith

TROMBONE

GRAND MARCH

from *Aïda*

Giuseppi Verdi
(1813-1901)
arranged by Walter Barnes

Grand March from Aida *continued*

THREE ELIZABETHAN MADRIGALS

I. My Bonny Lass, She Smileth

Thomas Morely
(1557-1602)
arranged by Walter Barnes

Three Elizabethan Madrigals *continued*

II. Come Again, Sweet Love

John Dowland
(1562-1626)
arranged by Walter Barnes

III. Now Is the Month of Maying

Thomas Morely
(1557-1602)
arranged by Walter Barnes

TRUMPET VOLUNTARY

John Stanley
(1713-1786)
arranged by Walter Barnes

Trumpet Voluntary *continued*

THREE SPIRITUALS

African-American spirituals
arranged by Walter Barnes

Three Spirituals *continued*

AMAZING GRACE

traditional American
arranged by Luther Henderson
adapted by Walter Barnes

TROMBONE